Where People Are Trees

Where People Are Trees

Poems by

Steve Minkin

© 2023 Steve Minkin. All rights reserved.
This material may not be reproduced in any form, published,
reprinted, recorded, performed, broadcast,
rewritten or redistributed without
the explicit permission of Steve Minkin.
All such actions are strictly prohibited by law.

Cover design by Shay Culligan
Cover art by Hugh Joudry
Author photograph by Ezra Distler

ISBN: 978-1-63980-236-4

Kelsay Books
502 South 1040 East, A-119
American Fork, Utah 84003
Kelsaybooks.com

To the many thousands of people who have touched my life.
To Moyna, Urmi, Joel and Martha. To my parents, ancestors
and the spirit of Odessa.

Acknowledgments

I am blessed with friends who do not hesitate to read my poems, often in their earliest embryonic states, nourishing them with feedback and me with encouragement. First and foremost Arlene Distler, along with Wendy Redlinger, Louise Rader, Charles Monette, Boris Bruton, Tim Mayo, Pati Sato, Meg Baronian, and Jerry Levy.

I wish to thank Cynthia Emanuel for our lifelong friendship. Sajed Kamel for his gifts of poetry and translation. Stu Copans the first person to illustrate one of my poems. Terry Hauptman mystical sister. Toni Ortner for her support. Sawnie Morris for sharing her knowledge and love of poetry. Write Action for providing opportunities for creative writers in Southern Vermont to commune and share their work.

Contents

There Was the Word	13
A Vermont Cemetery	14
Trinidad de Cuba	15
Preserved in Ash	16
Taming Purgatory	17
Village	19
The Alchemist	20
Trance	21
My Yiddishe Mantra	23
Kindness	24
Where People Are Trees	25
Protection	26
Memory	28
Trees	29
Old Friends	30
10 Paramis 10 Haiku	31
Slow	33
A Vintage Friendship	34
Careful	35
Midtown Commander	36
Dragonfly on Cold Stone Cemetery Bench	37
A Miracle	38
Mud	39
Inspiration	40
When I think about the body	41
In Need of Translation	42
Poetry	43
The New York Times on April Fool's Day	44
Weighted Down	46
A Good Samaritan	47
Lesson 1	50
Morning Mirror	51

My Fly	52
e.e. cummings	53
Limitless	54
Pause	55
One Day in Sikkim	56
Careless	57
On Becoming a Hungry Ghost	58
Come Home	59
On the Edge of November Night	60
One Way is Life	62
When we die as Peter said,	63
Like Old Rice	64
An Ongoing Dialogue	65
Rebirth	66
The Poet	67
Basho	68

There Was the Word

I sympathize with Lord Brahma
sitting alone,
stuck in emptiness
a writer's block so severe
trillions and trillions of years
unable to create *was, is* and *will be*
until he found the right word for OM

Yahweh built everything
the heavens and earth
night and day
oceans and dry land
creatures of the sea
terrestrial animals
birds in the sky
Adam Eve and the Garden of Eden
that said it took all of Genesis and most of Exodus
for him to finally dictate ten simple commandants

suffused as they are with sophomoric idealism
the Commandants are seen today as self-serving
forgettable   even dangerous
but as the sting of the bee protects the honey
these prosaic pronouncements
paved the way for the resplendent haiku of Jesus

do unto others
as you would seek to have done
lovingly to you

among the ruins of the Colosseum
the Roman orgy turned to love
lambs nibbling on flowers
sat with lions from Africa
where the poetry of thousands of unwritten languages is spoken

A Vermont Cemetery

4/7/20 (Early Covid)

on this early spring day
when so many corpses
have nowhere to go
facemask draped around my neck
a sign of the fear
in a breezy graveyard
where I come to refresh
my silhouette on stones

Trinidad de Cuba

blessed by a Santeria priest
bursting with joy
on a hot Cuba day

sun white as snow
water sprinkled on me
a gift from toiling African ancestors
who carried cobblestones
cut sugarcane

it was magic kindly bestowed
in a place where the night before
animals were sacrificed
blood still on the floor

what happens to ecstasies gone by
dreams lived
rituals nearly forgotten

Preserved in Ash

4/1/20 (Early Covid)

the day Wantastiquet
erupted
it covered Brattleboro in ash so deep
one thousand years later
everything about the material world we lived in
was preserved
that is the pots, pans, chairs and tables kind of stuff
in house after house people were buried in front of computers and
giant TVs
a thousand years ago screens froze on Fox CNN and MSNBC
when it was clear the end was near
at the time of the massive explosion and greatest fear
we perished separate and alone
having forgotten how to touch

Taming Purgatory

warned by the head of the department
this class is particularly difficult
one may hurl curses at you
thoughts of a burly guy
to my surprise
she had to go
we compromised
two young women
two cursing ladies
asked for passes to the library
I readily agreed
hopeful I would not see them again
Om shanti shanti
babysitter
brats
more than an hour left
useless waste of time
this Algebra 1

I am reminded of Southern Colorado
heading out with Chicano horsemen
into the *Sangre de Christo* mountains
to bring back cattle grazing there all summer
one horse had to be broken on the trail by a skilled rider

we rode for hours until we reached a high meadow
not an animal to be seen
the riders began shouting and whistling
the cattle grazing all summer knew the drill
coming down from the forested hillsides
all but one accounted for

on the way back my saddle-sore legs chafing in pain
but every moment was thrilling
moving the cattle along

fording streams
it was heaven
riding with real horsemen
what a memory to return

half hour to go
9th grade algebra
only one student in class to learn

I remember being the class clown
at the induction center in Denver
we were herded like cattle in a stockyard
fresh meat to send to Vietnam

we were ordered to take a processing exam
I refused to cooperate
disrupting the classroom
I resisted and protested this ugly war
using the very tools I had honed on substitute teachers

twenty more leaden minutes to go
chafed legs saddle sore pain
I dwell on the past
they are fully present

retreating into writing poetry
they sense victory
having no idea of how much I enjoyed this escape
there are times to assert control
and times to let go

they are as happy in triumph
as I am tickled by the gift of this poem

Village

    Mymensingh, Bangladesh

I went to a village far away
where time turned upside down
to hear you
and learn your wisdom
and you answered with strong winds and clouds
but little rain

We travelled by cycle-van over
a long dusty road,
Night
entered the stage
on the way to *Putijani*

The moon was full
but cloud hidden,
trees and houses
shown black in the horizon
our driver struggled
four wheels embraced the deep dry silt
bird sounds
and wind
and then from the opposite direction
the moan of buffalo carts straining
under loads of wood
destined for distant cremation

Perhaps no answer is simple
only patience and a willingness to see and hear
for long the wind blows empty
but much later
as we slept,
Putijani was blessed with a rich, drenching rain

The Alchemist

Jamalpur, Bangladesh

losing my way in the dark
as night fell
I stepped up to my thighs
into a pile of
human waste composting beside a fishpond

the pond was one of a dozen
bursting with life
cultivated by an unrecognized master
a man who turned desolate wasteland into a cornucopia
fruit trees and gardens
on the banks of ponds
teaming with fish

it was at a time and place
cursed by famine,
people were starving
when he first observed carts laboriously hauling
night soil to be dumped a mile or more beyond
the government fish farm
he came to manage,
where he was expected to write reports
draw a salary
accomplish little

Instead he created fertilizer
an odorless black powder
nutrition for plants and fish
an inexhaustible source of wealth
a defiant statement of the possible

Trance

    Bali, Indonesia

when the conditions are right
it will happen to you
when the gamelans play
it's something you don't question nor
desire
it happens when everyone moves out of the tent to the road
and the gamelans are playing
a person falls suddenly then another and another and another and
another
men women young old
makes no difference

can you imagine,
someone no longer here
the person's whole spirit pushed inside your body
how would that feel
or a spirit without human shape form or experience
makes no difference
the spirit uses you to dance
during the trance
your body a vessel
inhabited by a being
from another realm

called by the sounds of the gamelans
a spirit finds you
wanting to dance
you struggle
angry
resist the invasion
but in the end vanquished
it is no longer your body

impervious to blades or pain
stronger than any human
even knives pressed on your eyeballs can't hurt them
your possessed body dances
all night

when the sun comes up
you rise
from a deep sleep
refreshed
awakened by the sound of waves
and the shouts of fishermen pushing their boats into the ocean

My Yiddishe Mantra

I was born for this time with my mother
To be with her
During wheelchair yoga
Rehabilitation
Traveling thousands of years from India to a Long Island nursing home

Breath
Beautiful prana
Feeling breath   That white light helps you—in your body

Old people yoga
Take out your chin to stretch
Take in energy

Feel the strength of the earth
Making you well and able to walk again
Lift your toes if you can
Make space for new thoughts and new ideas
Feeling your toes receiving the gift from the earth

Feel the music   Every note a sacred mantra
Deep healing subtle energy bodies
Mother to son   son to mother

An Avatar at 93
She makes all who meet her happy

Culture note: The poem refers to "My Yiddishe Momme" debuted by Sophie Tucker in 1925. The song went on to sell millions of copies worldwide and not surprisingly was banned by the Nazis.
How few were her pleasures, she never cared for fashion's styles
Her jewels and treasures she found them in her baby's smiles
Oh I know that I owe what I am today
To that dear little lady so old and gray
To that wonderful yiddishe momme of mine

Kindness

when I think about kindness somehow Jesus comes to mind
I am not and never will be a Christian
in the formal sense
when I think of kindness somehow butterflies come to mind
I will never be a butterfly
that is in the formal sense
it is not that butterflies are particularly well known for kindness
but they are not cruel
when I think about kindness
I think about the Black women who tended to my mother the day
before she died
my dying mother said, I love you
and they joyfully replied
I love you, too

Where People Are Trees

    Chiapas, Mexico

white horses held at a police checkpoint
where is it
close to the border with Guatemala

which way to turn
there was a revolution here in a land where people describe
themselves as trees

the canopy heaven
the roots
the underworld we came from
the trunk is what we see

my dear friend is a sick tree
his brain radiated at the Mayo Clinic

what do we call trees escaping violence who are arrested at the
borders?

another thing they say
is I give my heart to you
for thank you

white horses held at a checkpoint
white clouds float everywhere

Protection

This blessing will make you safe
from earthquakes to dandruff
from a car accident and paralysis
to forgetting a name
from hurting
and forgetting
from losing and winning
from misspelling bicycle in a classroom
mistakenly giving a traveler wrong directions
from failing to withdraw when she says stay
from exhilaration and depression
from memory
from the heat and the cold
from being alone when you're dying
among loved ones distracted by their cell phones
from starts that never finish
from raindrops that begin as poems
joining other raindrops
as they rush down hills to
rivers joining other rivers
filled with fish and mud washing to the sea
to make you safe from tsunamis and blossoms
from the love you want to escape
the love you wish you could have
from her leaving you for the woman you trusted
to her returning again and again
only to end
from becoming a refugee or a lonely tourist in the wrong place
from always being late or simply never on time
from not looking good in the mirror
to failing to make an impression
for saying please and thank you too often
being unwelcoming
to someone close
or a stranger in need

thank you monks
every day this blessing lived and accepted

Memory

the poem came to me
in a poem fertile forest
but I had neither paper nor pen
there were trees in twos and threes
some conversed while others
connected like lovers frozen in time
some dead some dying

in the evening
I remembered
a white birch riddled with holes
this brought to mind
a beautiful old woman
I had seen long ago
her look of terror
carried by her sons on a cot
as they raced against death
for her to die on the shores
of a sacred river
by the cremation pyres
so her soul would rise
in the smoke of hallowed flames

Trees

it was as if I were walking
into a mouth and trees
were teeth rotting and regenerating
the wind   breath
the end day sun a watchful eye
the poet a morsel about to be swallowed

burned near the roots, she spawned
a lover in midlife
before rising to the top

some would say their roots were always one
they grew together
although the first branch
died after failing to reach her
others higher up now finger her bark as they tree talk in the breeze
they are after all the undisputed canopy for this patch of forest
neither the sun nor high flying hawks can tell them apart

dead branches sprout
like frozen climbers
resting in a crevasse
a tree once
so high and mighty
was no match for the rain and wind

Old Friends

we even shared cups of Sabbath wine
spent time at the beach
playing on the water
did magic
he'd cure the blind and cripples
raise the dead
I tried my hand at card tricks
but was never very successful
that was before he started having run-ins with the law
by then we hadn't seen one another for a while
I'm sure he still loves me
we're old friends

10 Paramis 10 Haiku

Generosity

Jerry's open house
cash for poets and musicians
cheese pasta cake wine

Virtue

waiting for the bus
he was held during the war
patience then and now

Renunciation

having seen war dead
the light outside has no flame
the world is within

Discernment

a fork in the road
every moment twists and turns
walk tarry or hide

Equanimity

calm and quiet mind
no judgement grasping nor fear
happiness follows

Patience

a terrible time
pregnant possibilities
many lives wasted

Persistence

Black Lives Do Matter
create love resolve sustain
we shall overcome

Truth

we gardened kindness
despite the vastness of time
as if it mattered

Determination

walking our first steps
we inevitably fall
as parents delight

Goodwill

find joy in others
neither trick nor deceit
smile with open eyes

Culture note: *Paramis* are enlightening qualities in Buddhist traditions.

Slow

It's just easier to go slow at my age
I know that's an unfair advantage
but one earned over time
an accumulation of interest
above and beyond wealth of experience
be patient, you can't rush slow
really slow

A Vintage Friendship

(to Boris)

it seems our friendship has become rather prosaic
gone are the dreams of burning down draft boards and revolution
or waiting for the state trooper to pass so we could join the seekers of
Sunday wine
or for that matter reflecting on how to do a headstand against the wall as described in
Ernest Wood's Yoga book
hitchhiking from San Luis, Colorado to Washington in solidarity with the DC Nine
nuns and priests
who poured blood over Dow Chemical files to protest the cruelty of Napalm
more prosaic even than your pestering about my failure to use the subjective with every Spanish phrase
yes, support socks reaching to the knees
a radical statement amidst a pandemic
Black Lives Matter
Trump
and the raging incontinence of the elders

Careful

In a small park
where homeless people
hang out
several benches
some grass
a shopping cart
perfectly packed
organized
by a skilled homemaker
someone who clearly cares
about the efficient
use of space
(perhaps an ex-marine)

Midtown Commander

she is the star of the show—2nd Avenue and 59th St.
just before the turn to Roosevelt Island
she keeps the traffic moving
the intersection clear with confident gestures
and her husky voice

Dragonfly on Cold Stone Cemetery Bench

morning—a cool August
Jewish Cemetery
stones on top of stones
marking visits
Martin is here
June 11, 2005

the cold evening
may have killed the dragon fly
but perhaps as the sun warms the stone bench
it may come alive
as Marty did for me this morning
somehow, someway

without ceremony
just now
the dragonfly
lifts into the air
disappearing against the background
of wet grass

A Miracle

10/20/21

momentarily blinded
a fuel truck traveling 80 miles per hour
pushed us from behind
I had slowed then stopped
in the passing lane
to avoid hitting phantoms in the dark

no longer believing what I see
betrayed by unfaithful eyes
unscratched but in shock
the crumpled car abandoned
we rented another
our destination not met

Mud

In this season of quicksand
setting traps for unsuspecting cars
you make clay into anointing vessels
and cups to drink tea
little remembered by history
mud features prominently in the nightmares of old soldiers
but was silk and satin
when we played naked
next to a river
overflowing with life

Inspiration

the story begins at the end of summer when
the smell of skunk is strong in the air
and the certainty of rain close at hand
it is a moment of peace

I want to talk to a dead friend
to bring him up to date
this time he could not have imagined

the pebble I place on his gravestone
is quickly surrounded by a faint pattern of rain drops
we share a laugh
at my urgent need to pee
and an uncontrollable necessity
to write a poem
on a nearby stone bench
any poem
this poem

When I Think About the Body

I recoil at the thought of killing
Chopping the chick out of human life
Emptiness when dead, crumbled, flipped, flopped
The architecture of living is mind-boggling
What a joy
To be healthy for as long as we can
And worship all others
In shapes sizes ages
Different and the same as our own

Even our cancers are processes
Gone bad, Taliban-like
Bent, broken, mutated
One that kills or awakens

But this body divine
The mind
These fears
Our spirits
Sex and conception

To kill is,
To kill or harm others
Is too big

God-like-Death

In Need of Translation

She gave me two books
of her poetry
a Syrian woman
years ago in Paris
she was attractive
we were drawn

married with children
excellent English
we talked for hours   stayed in adjacent rooms
at the top of our small hotel
we shared a bathroom
she was afraid of the dark
kept her door ajar

she gave me her books
covers romantically surreal
years before the birth and death of
the Arab Spring

is there a place for poetry
amid unrelenting evil
barrel bombs   gassed children
cities in ruins
a balm of rhyme and harmony
for refugees
a future in the face of slaughter

Poetry

at a certain point poetry asks you to unmask yourself
to take off smiles   self-pity
to stand naked
to be poked   prodded
in a room of mirrors with turned back eyes
before your bones and
the lies of everyday existence
scattered like broken coffee cups
lying about a lynch post

at a certain point poetry asks you
why are you here
how much are you prepared to give up
how much are you willing to lose

The New York Times on April Fool's Day

April 1, 2004

I ran out of coffee filters

Oh my god
It's raining out and I am suffering from a rare hangover
not a big hangover but a bottle of wine left
at my exhausted apartment
was red-filled-thick, blood-like, old-blood

I needed a transfusion, something different
as night moved to morning hours, I consumed the bottle of wine

On the radio—Radio Free Brattleboro
Michael asks his guest, *What do you do when your spiritual,
religious tradition doesn't do it for you?*

I walked down the street
for the comfort of coffee and the morning paper
my fix with the New York Times

The April Fools Edition
stomach-turning photos
of dismembered employees of a security firm
hanging on a bridge over the Euphrates River
hanging charred among the joyous descendants of the start of
civilization
the descendants of Noah, Adam and Eve

The spiritual healer on the radio
talks about enjoying the richness of one's own traditions
We don't know where we are going but we have to get there

My coffee, "Hometown Brew"
The pot was empty
I had to wait

I returned to reading
about Fallujah and the deep hatred of Americans
there

On the radio, her voice transcendent, the guest asks, *What is worse than Death?*

Birth

Weighted Down

on this near perfect day alone on a country road another week of mindless killings shall i praise the peace of spring in nature in my heart shall i grieve shall i watch the birds at play before the nesting begins feel the sun on my back hear the sound of water gently running into a ditch causing no harm shall i pray for liberation amid annihilation counting my blessings with such grief at hand

A Good Samaritan

in the pouring rain
just outside the bus shed
a white-haired gentleman approaches

what do you think?
should I call for help?

yes, I reply
keep him entertained,
inside the bus shed
an incoherent person covered in filth lies crumpled in a corner
my efforts at communication go nowhere

the Good Samaritan returns
I was released Monday from a psychiatric hospital,
they cannot hold people more than 10 days

I have no immune system
these blotches on my arms are from antibiotics
he suffers from repeated bouts of *pseudomonas pneumonia*

paramedics arrive
and began preparing the incoherent man before placing him on a gurney

I was raped as a child have PTSD
laid me out on the ground at my parents' place
raising his arms wide over his head spread-eagle

a paramedic
walks over asks him
how you doing?
been sober 10 days

*I jumped off the ninth-floor balcony but somehow they caught me
on the 8th*
these guys saved my life many times

played hockey in Canada
but the alcohol got too bad
worked in a steel mill
my lungs got too bad

two friends committed suicide
no one knows why
gesturing how one shot himself
a bullet under the chin

*my daughter and her husband live in Vermont.
they have lots of guns
she has an AR-15.
they won't see me no more
tell you the truth I'd rather be dead
what they said was so painful*

How you paying?
cash, I reply
he pulls out two cards from his wallet
giving me one

*I was going to move into rehab
but they won't take me because of my health*
pointing to his lungs
they hurt really hurt

60 years old
owes more than $250,000
in medical bills

I want to tell you a little joke about my bad memory

the bus arrives
he isn't getting on

we fist bump

do you need a transfer, the driver asks
his card it is good for three more trips

from my seat I wave back at him
trying to remember the joke about his bad memory

Lesson 1

taking my bicycle to the outer limits of where I could go by myself
even to run away before I got too hungry and returned home
I went to Valley Stream State Park and by a small stream I had my hideout with friends
but one day nestled in a hole at the bottom of a tree
I found a bottle with a magazine inside
a magazine with girlie pictures of women undressed to their bras and underwear
I could exaggerate and say yes this was my downfall
it certainly changed my adventures in nature searching for tadpoles, newts, eels and small fish
perhaps only my introduction to large land snails in a wood behind a friend's home could equal the thrill but that thrill was lost
as the land snail's habitat was devastated by the electric company clearing the area for a transformer
I loved finding praying mantis cocoons behind what is now a dry cleaner
I would hatch them either at home or in school
and then at some point one mantis would take off the head of another
more than a half a century later
I found out this is how they have sex
the female devours her lover's head and so he copulates endlessly even after death
I had no idea how far sex would take me past tadpoles, newts, eels and small fish
or upon returning the magazine to the bottle if I would ever find it again

Morning Mirror

I bet your mirror waits impatiently for you to wake
I bet electrons stir when water splashes your face
glass nearly exploding as you apply eyeliner
earrings playfully set
I bet something of you remains held by the mirror
as it does with me every time I see you

My Fly

It took a while as my anger diminished, that is the unfocused anger, the background noise of my life, for me to recognize the housefly taking shelter in my warm apartment in November was actually, rather than a pest, a stray catlike animal that came to me as a pet. So now I delight as the fly buzzes around me, landing on me and my computer screen, following me to the kitchen, bathroom and bedroom, my fly is my pet and perhaps overtime it will teach me something and perhaps out of love I will give her a name.

e.e. cummings

i feel like biblical Job
tormented by God
insomnia
up all night
tested beyond reason
for no reason,
i am reminded of the poet
e.e. cummings
who wrote, (always in lower case)
"the lord in his wisdom made the fly but then forgot to tell us why"
as i ponder the dreams owed me
the dreams lost

Limitless

(for Vinoba and Brian)

I saw with my own eyes
the vastness of my ignorance
before I knew
before I forgot
before a laughing sage

sparkling laughter filled the hall
the curtain disappeared
day became night
for a moment
I could see how far I could not see

day returned
I felt love
I felt loss
there was a larger lesson to be learned
being a young artist
I could not grasp its full meaning

the colors spread more slowly now
has the canvas grown
or am I smaller

Pause

in the real world there is gravity and bone against bone
in the other computer cell phone internet
the balance or better said the imbalance between chintz coming in
and going out
the seesaw heavily weighted in favor of the fat guy
in one world I am failing
absent backbone
in another I pause in bright daylight,
like the Zen master chased by a tiger
to a precipice
above a river filled with crocodiles,
clinging to a branch
he spies a ripe juicy berry   delicious

One Day in Sikkim

I was told to cut a lock of my hair
and place it on the ground
I was told to clip my fingernails over the hair
I was given a box of matches to light the hair on fire
I then warmed my hands and bowed over the burning remnants of
my body
I then placed my elbow in a rocky elbow notch
and cured my knees in a notch for knees
I pressed my ears against a wall of stone
that literally spoke in a language of stones
I squeezed into a narrow cave
crowded with pilgrims praying before a vagina
created by geological forces on a wet rockface

Careless

while in the depths of meditative intensity
in the hills above Singaraja, Bali
I thoughtlessly covered my body with a bucket of water
while bathing

as a result
of my inattention
a hopelessly light
large-shelled land snail
was flushed out the drain

today
nearly forty years later
after deciding to be
gentle with this day
I realized how much
that moment
still fills me with regret

On Becoming a Hungry Ghost

when the deeds are counted
the pluses and minuses weighed and balanced
if I left today
or tomorrow
amid mirrors facing yesterday in endless succession back and back
past lovers and haircuts
can't unpack can't undo
there are so many places I would do things differently
and others I'd die over and over for a chance to live again

Come Home

the ocean was strong today
the sky a turbulent fury
where is your pain?
why do you hurt so much?
your screams
come home mom
come home with me once again
let us forget all this

On the Edge of November Night

stopping by woods a stone cemetery bench
last light of an Iowa November day
Father your Thanksgiving death anniversary
so alert
in your death bed

we love you, we love you, we love you
the last words you hear
so important as you leave us
exiting the cold Bronx florescent light

moving on to eternity

He's dead—he's dead—he's gone, really dead, I softly tell mom
dead
a single tear grows and slowly runs down your cheek
a cheek known all my life
roughness felt as a child

you although dead acknowledge our last message
we love you, we love you, we love you
into eternity and
even in death you respond to our message of love with love
you give everything
even a moment of death's rest to return
love with love
by a simple tear

if all my life's work had the compassion of your last tear
your blessing will have been exalted
in heaven and earth

November spirit   departed
free in the universe well beyond the Long Island cemetery
your spirit travels the world with me
my guardian angel
blessed be he
who
a
January birth
protected and cared for us
even though his own childhood was denied

every day
a new year
Kaddish, Kaddish,
Yiskadal ve yis Kaddash
tears fall—*los muertos*
what a sky
a truly deathly honored sunset
in Iowa woods

Culture note: *Kaddish* is the Jewish mourner's prayer. This poem was composed for a Mexican *Day of the Dead* celebration.

One Way is Life

one way is life
the other death
the living force
the dying force
on most days the living force takes us with effort
to where we are going
on some days the strong winds of death push hard
until one day
we flow past the neck
beyond knowledge and sensation

When we die as Peter said,

A shroud has no pockets

Live today as if it is your last
Live today as if you will live forever
The Turkish taxi driver told me
on the other side of the Bosporus

The beautiful separation between East and West
Did you say, 'Life and Death?'

In a small boat it can be crossed in half an hour
if the wind permits
by ferry less

Sometimes even an hour will not suffice
to cross by car,
still faster a suicidal leap
off the bridge

A shroud has no pockets
what will Jeff Bezos do?
will he pay taxes upon his death?

What if he is born again in human form
cradled by a Guatemalan woman
thin breasts nuzzled as he drinks from a plastic bottle

Like Old Rice

like old rice
sitting in the fridge too long
even the best of oils
and vigorous stir frying
cannot improve the taste

there comes a time to throw out
old rice
even when it was
cooked with loving care

in cool morning sunlight
tender shoots are bundled

paddy
painfully transplanted
mulched   weeded   watered
harvested
dried   winnowed   bagged
and sold

on the stove
a fresh pot of rice boils

four chop sticks and two bowls wait

An Ongoing Dialogue

little shifts
perhaps a small toe
dipped differently
softly steamed
chopped carrots
so tasty
why intrude
I am nearly walking on water
living on carrots alone

the *Bodhisattva*
steps into this beautiful day
knowing the scale of pain in the world
the suffering of innocents
the dimensions
of misery
the amber caste of white privilege

acorns fall from above
seabeds rise from below
chop slice
chew

Rebirth

When I closed my poet's mind
it seemed like the
right thing to do
then I closed my poet's heart
blinded by ambition and
everyday life

and so I missed the ducks
on the river in winter
magnificent stalks of grass
holding seeds in the November sunlight
my heartbeat
the joy within my sadness.

with a closed poet's heart we made love
doors opened
bells rang
a friend appeared
to meditate on a river island
and on a far bank   I allowed myself to write this poem

The Poet

we were drops in a pool
vibrating to the sounds of her words
sharing a destiny be it the heavens or the seas
replenished by hope
her book grasped in salutation
who is this for, she asked?
an unmet soulmate, I replied
then let this be an introduction, she delighted
scribing your name

Basho

I want to be like Basho
in the heart of poetry
wandering the land
listening to water running
after days of rain
among the shadows of trees
among fish eluding nets

About the Author

Steve Minkin has worked on floodplain ecology, public health, and nutrition over decades. He is a researcher, historian, language interpreter, writer of nonfiction, fiction, and poetry. He lives in Brattleboro, Vermont.

www.ingramcontent.com/pod-product-compliance
Lightning Source LLC
Chambersburg PA
CBHW030914170426
43193CB00009BA/842